POLLUTION
PROBLEMS MADE BY MAN

NATURE BOOKS FOR KIDS
Children's Nature Books

What is pollution? Do people create all of it? Let's dig in to this dirty topic!

Mt. Etna volcano eruption and lava flow in Italy.

NATURAL AND UNNATURAL POLLUTION

Our air and water, and even the ground under our feet, can get filled with things that shouldn't be there. When that happens, we talk about pollution.

Volcanoes spew debris and ash into the air, plants let pollen fly, and cows create a lot of methane gas! But these kinds of pollution are part of the natural rhythm of life on our Earth.

What causes more worry is the dirtying of our air, water, and soil by the actions of people. Human-caused pollution can have long-lasting effects, not just on the health of people but on the health of the whole planet.

Let's look at some examples.

Air polluting factory chimneys.

IN THE AIR

Most worrisome air pollution is the result of human activity. We burn things for heat and power, ranging from campfires and wood stoves to huge power plants burning coal. These processes emit gases like carbon monoxide and carbon dioxide, and fine particles of many different compounds. Most cars and trucks burn gasoline, emitting both heat and gases. Businesses like dry cleaners and flour mills let both chemicals and particles of poisonous compounds into the air.

These processes contribute "greenhouse gases" to the atmosphere. These gases prevent the heat of the Earth from dissipating through the atmosphere into space. Some greenhouse gases are a good thing, but the level has gotten so high that the planet is warming as never before in recorded history. Read the Baby Professor book *What Every Child Should Know about Climate Change* to learn more about global warming and what we need to do about it.

Global warming from carbon dioxide.

On top of this everyday activity, there are frequent disasters that can cause a sudden surge in pollution. Here are some examples:

FIRE AT AL-MISRAQ

A sulphur plant near Mosul, in Iraq, burned in 2003, releasing 21,000 tonnes of sulphur dioxide, the largest release in human history, into the atmosphere. The fire, which burned for a month, may have been started on purpose.

Heavy burning fire.

BHOPAL

A pesticide plant in Bhopal, India, leaked poisonous gas in December, 1984. Over two thousand people died from the gas, and over half a million were exposed to it, some with long-term health effects. This was the worst industrial disaster the world has seen.

View of New Arif Nagar- a water polluted community from the chemical waste of the Union Carbide gas plant in 1984, in Bhopal - India.

THE GREAT SMOG

In 1952 a blanket of smog covered London, England for five days. Thousands died, mainly the elderly and those who already had respiratory diseases, and hundreds of thousands became ill. As many as 12,000 people died earlier than they otherwise would have because of breathing the poisoned air. Coal-burning factories and power plants were the main source.

Abandonded Battersea power station in London.

Water pollution in river because of industrial waste.

IN THE WATER

Here are examples of the way humans pollute both freshwater in lakes and rivers, and the oceans themselves.

CYANIDE SPILL

In 2000, in Romania, over 100,000 cubic meters of water contaminated with cyanide leaked out of a dam. Not only were 100 people sent to hospital because of eating fish contaminated with cyanide; thousands of fish and a huge amount of aquatic plants were killed.

EXXON VALDEZ

An oil tanker, the Exxon Valdez, ran aground off Alaska in 1989. It leaked as much as 750,000 barrels of crude oil into the sea. The spill caused immediate deaths to otters, seabirds, bald eagles, whales, and countless numbers of fish, and the effects of the pollution continue to be felt in the area.

Crab covered in crude oil from oil spill.

FLOATING GARBAGE

Plastic is everywhere. We use it all the time, and each of us throws out huge amounts of plastic in the course of a year. A lot of this plastic finds its way into the ocean, and a huge amount has formed a floating garbage pile covering hundreds of thousands of square miles of the Pacific Ocean.

This huge mess, which poisons the water as the plastics break down and causes dangers for animals and fish that accidentally eat some of the plastic, is called the Pacific Gyre Garbage Patch.

EXPLODING CHEMICAL PLANT

A series of explosions rocked a chemical plant in Jilin, China in 2005. Six workers died and thousands of people had to flee their homes. The chemicals released during the explosion, including tons of benzene and similar chemicals, leaked into the Sonhua River. Exposure to these chemicals can lead to leukemia.

A large amount of trash polluting the water.

DEEP WATER

In the Gulf of Mexico, an oil platform called Deep Water Horizon caught fire, exploded, and eventually sank in 2010. Almost five million barrels of oil were spilled into the ocean, smoke and gases from the fire caused health issues on land, and countless fish and seabirds died. That part of the Gulf of Mexico continues to suffer the effects of the disaster.

Explosion of an offshore oil and gas production platform.

AMOCO CADIZ SINKING

The Amoco Cadiz, a huge oil tanker, ran aground and broke apart off France in 1978. When it sank, it released over 1.6 million barrels of crude oil into the sea. This resulted in a huge loss of marine life.

A DEAD ZONE IN THE GULF OF MEXICO

The Mississippi River carries down to the Gulf of Mexico huge amounts of nitrogen and phosphorus. These substances come from fertilizers used across the United States, that are washed into the great river system. These substances have caused a *"Dead Zone"* where fish and marine plants cannot survive at the mouth of the river.

MINAMATA DISEASE

Minamata Disease comes from extreme mercury poisoning, and attacks the nervous system. It is named after Minamata Bay in Japan, where, in 1956, a company released waste water containing high concentrations of methylmercury. Over 2,000 people died because of the pollution, and many more were crippled for life.

Water pollution.

Toxic and chemical waste found illegally dumped in MABPAI area

ON THE GROUND

Pollution on the ground includes our huge garbage dumps, which leak toxic materials into the soil as well as providing a home for large populations of disease-carrying rats. Here are some examples of the way we have polluted the ground:

THE LOVE CANAL

In New York State in the 1940s, chemical companies buried hundreds of tons of toxic waste in the neighborhood of Love Canal, near Niagara Falls. Nobody told the residents, as the community grew, that many homes were built right on top of the toxic waste. The pollution led to high rates of cancers, birth defects, and miscarriages, and is a symbol of our failure to care for the health and safety of the generations that follow us.

Plastic containers and garbage lying on chemical contaminated waste land.

WAR IN KUWAIT

During the war with Iraq, which had invaded Kuwait, in 1991, 600 oil wells were set on fire by the Iraqis as they retreated. It cost over $1.5 billion to put out the fires, and the oil and other materials caused heavy pollution to the ground over a wide area.

A BOMBER CRASHES

In 1966, a US bomber crashed near a small village in Spain. It carried non-nuclear bombs, but also an amount of plutonium, which is highly radioactive. The pollution of the area is still evident today.

SIDOARJO MUD FLOW

In Indonesia, a mud volcano was stimulated in 2006 by the blowout of a gas well drilled nearby. The volcano has been erupting constantly since, sending out a huge amount of mud which covers fields and former villages. It is expected to continue erupting for the next thirty years.

FOLIAGE DESTRUCTION

During the Vietnam War in the 1960s and 1970s, the United States dosed large areas of Vietnam with herbicides. They wanted to cut down on forested areas where enemy fighters could prepare for attacks. This action also destroyed food sources for people and animals across a wide region of Vietnam, and the land has not yet completely recovered.

ELECTRONIC WASTE

There is a huge dump of electronic equipment in Guiyu, China—broken computers, outdated batteries, and worn-out computer monitors. Lead and other materials leak into the ground and from there to the water supply. Over 80 percent of the children in Guiyu suffer from lead poisoning, and there is a high rate of miscarriages.

Nuclear power plant.

OTHER POLLUTION

Here are some other examples of the way human action has polluted our planet.

THREE MILE ISLAND

Three Mile Island was a United States nuclear reactor in Pennsylvania. It suffered a partial meltdown in 1979. Small amounts of radioactive gas and iodine were released into the air, and the country narrowly avoided a huge disaster that would have followed if the reactor had experienced a complete meltdown.

ASBESTOS CONTAMINATION

In Libby, Montana, many people worked in the vermiculite mines. However, many workers and local residents became sick because the mining company made high use of asbestos, which is highly toxic. Contact with asbestos can lead to a range of serious diseases. The mines started operation in 1919, and asbestos pollution of the area is extensive.

Asbestos chrysotile fibers that cause lung disease, COPD, lung cancer, mesothelioma.

CHERNOBYL

In Ukraine, the nuclear reactor at Chernobyl experienced a serious "nuclear event" in 1986. Many people died from radiation exposure, and large section of the country is not habitable even today.

Chernobyl atomic electric power station.

Save the world. Paper cut of Green city concept on green grass.

HEALING OUR
EARTH

All people must work together to keep from hurting our home, the planet Earth. Read the Baby Professor book, *Mother Earth Needs a Band-aid!*, to learn more.

Visit
BABY PROFESSOR
EDUCATION KIDS
www.BabyProfessorBooks.com
to download Free Baby Professor eBooks
and view our catalog of new and exciting
Children's Books